You've Changed

JONATHAN BYRD

Thank you to Corin Raymond, Eva HD, Rob McMaken, Alison Moore, and Alan Gann for their help editing and assembling this collection of poems.

CONTENTS

III. DRIVER

IV. HOLY WATER

1. Eden

judgment is a curse
the story of the garden
the first sin: knowledge

NOD

Cain was the first homeless man.

He chose the wrong profession and it displeased the LORD. He became a soldier and killed his brother in the first bloody revolution. The LORD awarded him a life sentence of unwanted freedom.

He came to dread the nights sleeping on the concrete. It hurt his back, his ass, and his arms. In the daytime he hiked around the city hauling a backpack in the desert heat.

Cain's mother could never forgive him. She lit a candle every night for Abel. He would have been a good father, She said.

God protected Cain. Perhaps it was the first time He walked around in a man's skin, in order for His words to have weight.

Cain was a sharecropper, a farmer without a farm, his brother's blood in his red-rimmed eyes. Sweet fruits reminded him of his own long ago. It was no camping trip. It was the beginning of an experience.

He too remembered his brother, and it shamed him. The fat of the firstlings. The respect of the LORD. The Almighty Dollar.

Cain filled a small blue backpack and left his apartment. A thin sleeping bag. A few books. A ski mask. Baby wipes.

He thought about his failed farm. The crumbling barn. The sinking tractor. The noose in the tree. His face as abandoned.

He had no toothpaste. Thirty-five dollars.

God said, Why the long face?

Satan thought the whole thing was a bad idea. You give him a temporary Hell? I want a temporary Hell.

God said, Don't listen to him. Those who do well will be accepted. Those who do not do well will sin as you have.

God's mind was fixed. Many of His congregation were living in poverty. His church was young.

Abel always told me what to do, said Cain. I couldn't take it anymore.

I love you and I want to understand you, said God.

Satan came around to the idea and strove to be Cain's guide, telling him where to bed down at night.

God said to Cain, Where is Abel, your brother?

I don't know. I can't keep up with him.

That first night, Cain heard every siren. Every dog bark. Every foot fall. He hid himself behind a row of plastic trash bins in the back lot of a church. He slept on the concrete because he knew scorpions would be looking for water in the night.

God said, I want to believe you. I want you to tell me the truth.

The ground is very hard, Lord. My hands and arms keep falling asleep. The light is so bright I can't hide my face from it.

God said, Use your ski mask. Your brother's blood makes the ground infertile. You are a fugitive from yourself.

The following nights, sleep came easier because Cain was exhausted. He rode the bus. He walked for miles to find shade and food. The days became a wheel.

Lord, my punishment is greater than I can bear. I can't find you anymore when I pray. All I know is suspicion and hunger. I'm afraid someone will kill me.

Cain sat in the bus stop and waved at the drivers. He cleaned himself in the bathroom of a library and checked his email. No reply from God.

He sat under the trees of a courtyard and an old woman brought him some food. He walked downtown in the dry heat of the afternoon, the sun on his bent and balding head. He caught a bus back out to his sleeping spot and sat on a bench outside an auto shop until it was dark enough to hide again. The owner offered him the last of the coffee before he closed. Cain cried.

The owner of the auto shop thought Cain was insane and possibly dangerous. He set the styrofoam cup of boiled coffee outside the door. He bid goodnight from behind the stenciled window, switched off the last light, and locked up. He left out the back and drove in the other direction, circling the block to avoid even the crazy man's eyes. As if misfortune was contagious.

Cain still sought God. He read the Bible in the public library. He recycled the flotsam of the city.

God said, I was evicted from the earth by Man. My sacrifice will mean forgetfulness of Myself in man. It will mean entering into man's hopes and fears, his longings and despairs. Then I will build a new home in heaven.

Cain's red beard thickened. He found a hat in the trash and it fit him. He smelled strong.

God said, I will protect you.

FLASHLIGHT

You said I'd better take a flashlight.
I carried it down your driveway along the rapids of the river.
I set it on the table inside the guest cabin.
In the morning, I set it outside on the rocking chair on the
front porch.

I could have seen the gravel of your driveway.
The eyes of a raccoon. The darkness like horse blinkers
for people who might see the night and panic, or become
distracted from their course.

Distract me oh great void and heartache.
Leave me untethered
in the golden grass under a silver moon.
I break and run along the edge of the night.
The dark spine of the mountain.

I was up until the morning. I listened to music.
I sent bright sparks along a cable around the world.
I told my friends that I loved them.
I wrote bad poetry.

I wished the stars with me into the blinding day.
I poured the salt sea over the mountains.
I hid the night in my coat.
I kept a dark place inside me where the birds slept.

The fridge ran lonely in the kitchen.
The heat howled briefly against the eternal cold.
A car passed on the road outside.
I walked up to the house for breakfast,
which is always too early.

I know I am not alone.

Do you not love the night?
I take mine for long walks after everyone has gone to work.
The road is almost as quiet.

I pull the night from my coat and drape it over a power line.
I pretend I am drunk and have a great idea for a song.
If only the night would hold out.
If only the ocean would swallow the whole world.
I would go with Noah and be the whistling custodian of
nocturnal animals.

Noah would come out in his housecoat and tell me
I'd better take a flashlight.
I would walk off to feed the wood owl and the bat-eared fox
and the spectacled bear.

I would sing to the fireflies.
I would go out on the fo'c'sle and
chuck bobcat feces into the deep ruin of the world.

I would listen to the water splash on the bow
like the hushing rapids of this river
and wait for Noah to turn the lights out
so I could finally see.

down our short driveway
I walk across the morning
without spilling tea

SPRING COMEDY

I broke a bird glass
right in front of my wife
she wasn't surprised

a Carolina wren
laughed on the porch
teakettle teakettle

Frye said that spring
is comedy's turn
and I have to agree

beautiful girls and
young men with roses
blowing their noses

mated and married
father rain rages
the squire plows the mud

no longer under
the rustic illusion
love is the straight man

the singing of raptors
the shit on the flowers
the jogger's erection

the weeping of women
choking on pollen
in berry-stained dresses

you see what I mean
it seems formulaic
to the young ones archaic

but the ones who are oldest
are laughing the hardest
stop it you're killing me

the grassy graves growing
the gardener mowing
the plots where we're going

in the garden so formal
as if that were normal
in a world full of weeds

now we stand naked
as spring draws the curtains
and laugh with a passion

the winter defeated
old miserable miser
mocked and deserving

you see what I mean
it must be the spring
that cheapens possessions

the weedeaters whining
the dishwasher bleeding
the broken glass winking

she said I liked that one
but the one I miss most
is the tufted titmouse

our little boy laughing
the wren's wild whinging
teakettle teakettle

REAL

I said to God, Are you real?

God said, Does it matter whether I am real or not?

I said, Well I don't want to feel like a fool.

God said, Are you familiar with the fable of the fox and the sour grapes?

I said, Of course.

God said, Does it matter whether the grapes are real?

THOU LORD

Thou Lord. Multiply thy name
in this naked darkness.
Beasts living in the field.
Divide the dominion.
Let heaven multiply.
Make food.
Earth meat, fruit of the serpent.
Cursed garden.
As soon as man named the tree, the
heavens died. A creeping seed
in the Eden River grass.

There is a third voice.
East in the air.
Till in the morning,
eat in the evening.
Blessed is the herb garden.
Adam's flesh divided the waters.
Living is good.
Blessed rule the One-Three-Seven.
Form the flesh, divide and die.
Return to the firmament a taken thing.
A woman knows, a man learns.

The evening has eyes.
The creatures make dust.
First sorrow, then life.
Thou Lord.

II. Soft Tissues

Japanese beetle
on a wisteria bloom
I send you to Hell

TYRANNOSAURUS DOMESTICUS

They say there's a great deal in common
between a Tyrannosaurus Rex and a chicken,
though I wouldn't know because I
have never eaten fried Tyrannosaurus.

I can however corroborate
a chicken's cold-blooded terrible tearing
a small snake no-limb from no-limb,
and plucking the eyes from a blind mole.

We each must have plucky ancestors.
We all got small in our own way,
the feathered Tyrannosaur giving up flight
and thank God for that.

Even now, a cockfight is never over easy
and collecting eggs for the peckish can be risky,
your hard-won hand beneath the great tyrant-hen
when you realize she's turned broody.

I imagine all the little mammals
that survived the infernal meteor
picked their bones clean. Even then,
everything loved the taste of Tyrannosaur.

Now the skunks, weasels, and raccoons—
basically anything larger than a mole—
chew their way through chicken wire
just to rub it in.

I think sometimes I still see it,
the cold regard in a deposed red eye.
"I am still the King," it says.
"Someday I will reclaim my teeth."

SOFT TISSUES

I read they found the tail of a dinosaur
preserved in amber for ninety-nine million years,
sold as jewelry in a market in Myanmar.

Mosques were occupied by soldiers,
used as sites for rape or burned down.
Children were slaughtered with knives.

There were feathers like the chest feathers of a robin,
chestnut brown above and paler white beneath,
signaling from the Cretaceous like a frightened doe.

Sanctions have eased. The economy is developing well.
The country is rich in jade and gems, oil, and natural gas.
It is the largest producer of methamphetamine in the world.

The skin and muscle were reduced to a thin film of carbon
like a pencil mark on a climate map curving upward.
Time is not kind to the soft tissues.

Drift down the Irrawaddy River in an old steamer.
Enjoy the beach on the Bay of Bengal.
It's the dawn of a more democratic era.

We can see just how degraded the material is.
There is no way to bring it back to life.
A fossil is just an impurity to a jeweler.

Christians and Muslims cannot join the Army.
That privilege is reserved for Buddhists.
It is remarkable how things change over time.

OTHER GODS

I asked God once, What about those who worship other gods?

God said, There are no other gods.

I said, Why do they worship the wrong gods?

God said, That's not what I said.

UBUD

the lightning woke me
for a split second I saw
your towel on the door

thunder shook the house
the faint smell of coconut
you sighed in my ear

YOU'VE CHANGED

We had breakfast with a friend
it made us late for an appointment
but we got some great photos

I was reading the side of that building on Queen Street
when I stepped out in front of the bus
In letters three stories high
it said You've Changed

I have.

it's no surprise that your taste buds choose your mood
The softness of light saltiness
The pleasure of discovering everyone
The rare salvation of satisfaction

Mary Oliver said on the radio

There is no nothingness
but there might be an end to consciousness

That's why I shouted Thank You
in the middle of Queen Street
as I was about to die

just in case

Thank You

It was hard but in the end
I loved life
most of all I loved my senses
I had breakfast with friends
I'm ready again

Thank You

ZOMBIE

I was sitting in the rain in my car
you were dying of brain cancer
or not dying of brain cancer
depending on whether the cat is alive
when we open the box

Halloween night, I walked through the Field of Screams
a bloody bodiless leg lying in the path
a man with a banjo in the graveyard.
a corpse in the tree that came to life
nothing was as scary as brain cancer

it is a stage 3 cat
or maybe a stage 4 cat

the thing that nobody mentions is
the third option: the cat is not in there.
It's because there is no third option.
The cat cannot perform any of the more
famous tricks of quantum physics

a corpse cannot really come to life
not even on Halloween night

I turned the key and took you some soup
your head was stapled like Frankenstein
you hugged me and were not undead
maybe you were more alive than ever

I SING BEST WHEN I FEEL ANOINTED

God's not one to think aloud.
Sometimes she takes five minutes.
Genius is the patience
to outwit a dull moment.

I trust the unseen Creator
in your unfolding squash blossom,
what you feel, think, and know,
your leg, spine, and tongue.

I trust my holy instinct
as time steals my vision.
You are ancient as the ocean.
Pin me down and drown me.

The will to love survives
any one love and even life.
Every child is born a stranger.
Every prophet becomes a danger.

Even conversation is a competition
to know the world from all eyes.
Leave a trail for me
in your wilderness.

I'll drink your experiment.
I'll take your rejection.
I'll chant your beauty,
our enthusiasm alone a triumph,

every word an inspiration,
a revolution in God's mind.
When you are inaudible,
you will be my oracle.

loss of right ventri-
cular function is a strong
predictor of death

III. DRIVER

DRIVER

It was a loud banquet in O'Hare like any other. The gentleman parked the old black limousine at the airport and woke up his passengers. A wild dispatcher. A woman from the suburbs. The cat's name was Trooper.

Chicago residences are unique and special, each with their own back story. They are famous for their driving. The story goes, Billy Graham drove a young chauffeur to the wrong address, a bachelor party really.

Jesus, there are a lot of tolls.

The passenger sat outside. The supervisor took their badges thinking something horrible happened. Instead the driver rolled his dinner.

Got one? he asked.

You can't make this stuff true.

Five minutes, gentlemen. Outrageous. When I came here, everybody spoke English. Drivers. Passengers. Cops. Let's get going. I got one more pick-up.

UNTITLED-85

in creative mode
like a child
i can't find things on my computer

which is why i
opened the laziest app
I could get to
to write this

I'm not even rhyming
or anything.

The only thing
I'm not lazy about
is creating more poetry.

my desktop is full of poems
untitled
untitled-1
untitled-2

MOOSE JAW TO MEDICINE HAT

They say a bison will beat itself to death against a gate
that separates it from its mate or even a mangy horse
No beast is an island in this landlocked ocean of weeds
its windpumps watering waterless wales

Out where the prairie turns to plains
the trucks turned puddles into mad grey oceans and seas of
salt spread sterile broad and white like the blinding face Elijah
wrapped himself against

The fences grew sideways friendly to the wind
A sedan sat rusting to the handles in a cow pond

A gust pushed a semi somewhat into our lane
a double tanker of black snake bending
and we needed fire but not that much
then we saw pronghorns and all was right again

Trains carried trans Canadian graffiti across
pitiless plains, cityless signatures from cities unnamed
breaking the gates to be one with the wheat
and unknown to the law of wild rose country

EVERY DAY

I told God I was afraid.

God asked, What are you afraid of?

I said, I'm afraid I will not have enough.

God said, Here. Take this and you will never want again.

I said, It's very small. Is this all I need?

God said, It is.

I asked, What is it?

God said, Gratitude.

EXIT NOW

One looked west as far as Hickory. A flock of birds. We came
to this country when I first left the service. The day of the fire.
We left Egypt for Greensboro.

Exit for gas. Exit for food. Exit for your community.
The children welcome you, express lodging for a pharaoh.
Need water? Statesville, daughters.
Out of bondage? Rest area. Rock church. Downtown has the
best midwives.

Exit with the Yadkin River. Go like Moses, renegade son.
Mocksville needs you. Free their women. Israel, Catawba and
God camping.
Trucks deliver on the highway. I see the signs. Exit now.

One looked west as far as Hickory. A flock of birds. We left
Egypt for Greensboro. Food and lodging. Exit now.

THE NEW ONUS:
Embership Has Its Privileges.

What's up, kind globe?

us embers have access to a journey.
Regardless of level there's always free sage, as well as great
partners. Silver embers qualify for extra age. In addition,
embers get security when traveling—all you need is
God. Diamond embers have extra baggage and a larger onus.
embers are guaranteed a
departure. As a God ember, you can give to a family. Diamond
embers can make soon a God ember.

WHERE WILL YOU TAKE YOU?

SIGN UP FOR FREE
EARN POINTS
Did you know?
Now you can earn light.

ON, ON!
IN, IN!
NEW IS BEST!
NEW IS NICE.
AN OK CAN MEAN EVERYTHING!

Embers, partners, points on everything. More than air.
Combine your onus with "I can." Earn points when you hop.
Unlocking the benefits is easier than ever.

STAY CONNECTED

free everyone.
become more.

Start today!

they call me crazy
I just want to change the world
maybe on Wednesday

iv. Holy Water

the grain of lake ice
the old pine's darkened heartwood
polished by moonlight

THE BAPTISM II

The beginning of God;
written in your face
crying in the mountains,
baptize the mountains,
the land confessing.
hair, and skin and wild honey;
saying, I am not worthy.

water: the Holy Ghost.
the French Broad River.
like a dove descending
a voice saying, I am.

into the mountains.
with the wild beasts;
preaching the gospel
time is fulfilled.

into the sea:
Come you after me
Come you after me

SEVEN HORSES

Seven horses swimming
All granite head and mossy eyes
Eleven bands of ripples wake
Iron brown and veed like geese

They stop for a moment in slow unison
The ripples gather around them in circles
Stones in the gravel bed of a zen garden
Stopping for a thousand years to pay their respects
to their destination, as if reaching it would
relieve them of the struggle that they came for.
As if they have traveled this far to see God
and now they are afraid.

ANTHONY

Alexandria:
the desert is a city
emptied of desires.

Now that martyrdom is dead,
where is the prayer of the heart?

IN THE CITY

In the city,
it's rare to be naked
or wash dinner dishes.
Quiet is relative.

In the city,
lost men become beggars
or worse, so successful
they think they're above it.

I've learned not to look,
to carry a book.
I sift through people
to find what I need.

In the city,
there's a beautiful girl.
I rest in the garden
of her perfect plucked brow.

In the city,
it's rare to be naked
or wash dinner dishes.
Tonight's an exception.

ENDING

At night, in the fields, they saw a vast city. Current thought
had failed them. That which has appeared must be believed.
Devils rolled gently, loosened into obscurity. "Go" shook
their lips, the beat confirming heaven, every wasted unbelief
following together afterward. Heaven a blanket. Fingers like arms.

They pulled the tired hardness closer. New words wasted in a
deadly end. They stretched, moved looking across signs. Heads
still bared. Face beside wonder. Lord whispering. Somewhere, a
brooding God. Tongues stood to grasp a drink, hearts already
in the future.

Sick serpents from a dark world receded. Hands preached.
Came forth a wide thing. A lawn light. The hurt received
comfort. The old sat frightened.

The gospel cast tomorrow in a word, the republic risen from
the past, the creature to come. They rose from their boats,
unknown and no matter.

FAITH HEALING

There are signs scientists heal
according to the gifts of life
conventional miracles

God's ailments may be cured by faith
movement restored with intercessory prayer
a miraculous revival

among the cures, children of a higher Jesus
The ministry's authority over health
died, however.

HOLY WATER

Fishers, cast your net into the wild. Nets hold nothing.
God gathered the sea. God taught the water every way.
Many may make a kingdom, but none make a wilderness.

The beasts have authority. Did any man baptize a fish?
Did Satan cast his net into the sea? Repent indeed.
Even the priest is a kneeling servant to sin.

Seek inside you the sea, the watery wilderness.
Make peace with the fever, the mending blaze.
The wild scribes come, saying nothing forever.

v. Houses Know

you've been here before
you know the path in the dark
make yourself at home

MAKING THE BED

My mother taught me how to make the bed.
The Navy taught me how to make the bed.
My wife taught me how to make the bed.

It's like trying to bend a spoon with my mind.
I've seen people do it. I sit and stare.
I clench my teeth and wish.

But the spoon is whole. The top sheet is sideways.
There's a long ridge that I name many names.
The pillows look like a whorehouse.

Even a deathbed has hospital corners.
I'm a maid in my mother's own Hell.

REFLECTIONS ON
SOUTHERN GARDENING

Wisteria chinensis,
bane of my exensis.

PAINTING OF THE BAPTISM

Open scent-filled rich Christ, light the door that is so heavy.
Delicate pink-flowering lilac Jesus, summer garden of God,
perfume the beginning of this gospel with your Son.

Amidst the trees there came a wind.
Amidst the thorn came roses.

A cross voice murmurs at the front round window.
Prepare the burden. Prepare the way.
At the branches' insistence, the painters note.
The dim medium can hardly catch even a momentary sense,
pallid, innumerable, sullen, oppressive,
a gleam lying, crying like saddle-bags.
Behold, a dusty, distant Lord.
Behold, birds and bees circling in the stillness.
The effect is gilt with swiftness,
making the flamelike messenger roar monotonous stillness.

Art is immobile, a jade-faced organ.

Motion blossoms, producing fantastic curtains,
able beauty, tremulous and straight.
The honey-sweet wilderness, the one laburnum
to seek the unmown grass.

The horns huge, smoking.
Thy honey-coloured face.

Young and awake, the Lord went into the wilderness.
Years passed ever languidly across the river.
To preach was a pleasure.
To baptize the river.
To sudden sitting and
really strange dreams within extraordinary people.

The painter at his easel. Land and time.
Suddenly, skillfully, full-length form!
Beauty confessing to the vulgar!
The portrait seemed lovely, its sins in remission.
The face lingers upright!
As though to see its own lids.

HOUSES KNOW

Houses know.
Two people first thing make dust.
Mama like one day.
Kind trouble sky clouds.

Houses know.
Old children get time.
Country red face.
The last girls on Earth.

Things got daddy.
Lord, trouble now.
Go long, spear toward light.
Land, tree, fields.
Ask leaves.

Houses know.
School work.
Gray life toward green.
Tire far make dust.
Houses know.

charred in the fireplace
edges of torn out pages
a thrush's anvil

VI. UNSOLVED

UNSOLVED

Blood is black on the blade.
Grass is green on the grave.

SAFE PASSAGE

Now that I am free
I choose my own god
She is a mother God
who taught me how to run

A cougar can see your soul
like lightning in a cloud
you cannot hide
you might as well dance

If you can see my soul
you miserable son of a bitch
I'm dancing

I don't know where this is going
these damned exploding birds
like fireworks for dogs

If I am captured I just have to remember
how to be grateful for this freedom
I have right now

wisteria blooms
the killer's perfume lingers
trees strangled to death

A HOMELESS GOD

There's a hundred years.
There's a homeless God taken down from the sky.
Heaven made a name.
The face of Cain never aged, people say.

I'd like to live forever.
Surely there will be a day.
I'll get what I've got coming and pray like Adam prayed.

Who created died.
The people sang just to know they were the same.
In the widow's field,
the seed was bared to the flesh that lived again.

I'd like to live forever.
Surely there will be a day.
I'll get what I've got coming and pray like Adam prayed.

Life begat life begat
begat life begat
begat life begat
begat life

there's a hole in the ground
begat life begat
begat life
all the people throw
begat life begat
begat life
every thing ever made
begat life begat
begat life

well we called it home
begat life begat
begat life

There's a hundred years. There's a homeless God.

THE APOSTLE PAUL REPORTS ON
THE ELECTION RESULTS

Well-meaning trumpet, you killed woe for reason.
The Lord and locusts of Democracy have a lot to face tomorrow.
We felt. We believed. Is truth relative or absolute?
Journalism using horses was more efficient.

The number is cast. The dust from the battle pit in our mouths.
Are you surprised at death? The blood on the grass?
The star in heaven?
Now great darkness issues scorpions on the Earth,
brimstone, smoke, and breastplates of
bottomless angels.

Angels were bound and taken to war. They died a thousand times.
Policies have teeth. Party tonight, informed revolutionary.
Heaven was abandoned in fire. One day you'll be surprised.
Try as you might, you can't elect God.

VII. HEAVEN

from her Jovial eye
to her pedicured moon
what a stellar lady

THE ULTIMATE ARGUMENT

The ultimate argument
for the existence of the Earth
is that we all agree it is here.
It's not much of an issue
for scientists.

I've been living since facts
became passé and othered.
Others may report space
but what evidence do they offer?
I haven't been there.

Even if I created God in my brain
vainly gendered and vindictive
even if consciousness is brain activity
what then do we name the electrons
that dance on the head of a neuron?

Look I love serious medicine
the fact that I don't have polio
and survived my suicidal twenties
through the miracle of penicillin.

Science goes endlessly inward
and endlessly outward
but what with or without a name
goes endlessly onward?

The smaller we get
the less we know.
With nouns like eyebrows
the role of consciousness is
dubious at best.

I know this poem doesn't look big
but it holds the universe
the way theory does not.

EVERY MAN OLD GOD-BOY

Every man old God-boy. Earth day fish like dust.
Great corn even settled. Pale houses became morning.

Heaven people gone. Blanket leaves another lifted.
Country horses looked brown. Waters grew beer.
Gray days together around every fowl.
Sea bed women thin dry high. Make children.

Every man old God-boy. Sky father get old.
Saw two sea. Let home something called never.
Light came strong.

Heaven people gone. Net deep. Face spread.
Seen seed
borrow eyes. Many night little air. Man's crust.
Weeds moved.

Every man old God-boy. Told days around
evening.
Knew fields. Time made May meat. See across
terrace.
Fishermen.

Heaven people gone. Night took time. Fruit lay without
rain. Something called back. Never red land.
Eat tree herb. Sail yielding. Firmament carried clouds.

Every man old God-boy. Heaven people gone.

SO I CAN SLEEP

I like poets who swear
less is more
earthy abbreviations of long histories
with parents
with the world
with God dammit

I write things down so I can say them again

I like poets who obviously wash dishes
the sound of service in service to words
checking both sides of a sound
for anything that might send it back into the water

you write things down so you never have to say them again

I like poets who write short books so I can sleep

we are in heaven
the sky is an illusion
like any border